MOMMY SAYS NO

SELENA PYLE

ACKNOWLEDGEMENT/ THANK YOU

I would like to thank Kinetic Digital publishers for making this book happen and a special thanks to Steven Khan my account manager and Sarah Brown my project manager without their time and dedication this book would not have come together how I wanted . They spent hours and days making sure they got in contact with me and made sure I approved of the outcome. Thank you .

DEDICATION

I dedicated this book to my baby girl Sade Land. Mommy loves you. I made this book so you can have something to remember your childhood memories as we grow together. This is the first book dedicated to you. Much love from Mommy.

No !
MOMMY MOMMY MOMMY
Can I go out to play
WELCOME

No!
Mommy can I jump up here

Mommy can I play with this ?
No!

No!
Mommy can I open this ?
Soda

No!
Mommy can I touch The Pot ?

Mommy can I look at this
No!

No!
Mommy can I smell this ?

No!
Mommy can I taste this ?

CHARACTER ANALYSIS ACTIVITY

Why did mommy say no to going outside

____

____

____

____

____

____

____

CHARACTER ANALYSIS ACTIVITY

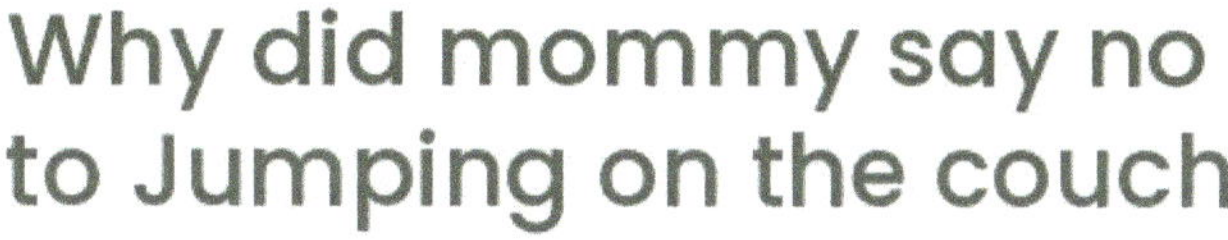

Why did mommy say no
to Jumping on the couch

____

____

____

____

____

____

____

CHARACTER ANALYSIS ACTIVITY

Why did mommy say no to touching the plug

____

____

____

____

____

____

____

CHARACTER ANALYSIS ACTIVITY

Why did mommy say no
to opening the can?

____

____

____

____

____

____

CHARACTER ANALYSIS ACTIVITY

Why did mommy say no to touching the pot

____

____

____

____

____

____

____

CHARACTER ANALYSIS ACTIVITY

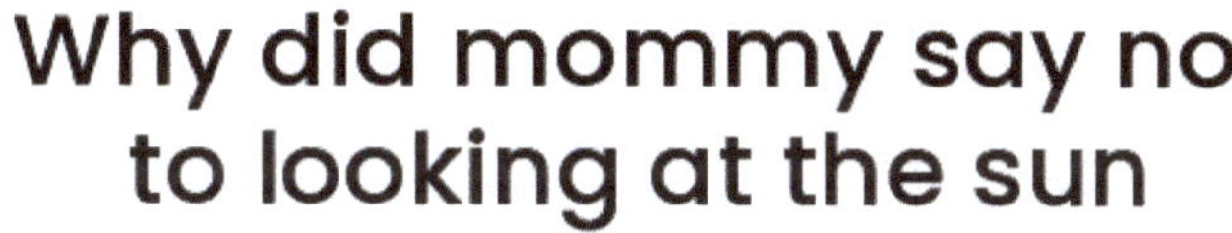

____

____

____

____

____

____

CHARACTER ANALYSIS ACTIVITY

Why did mommy say no to smelling the perfume?

____

____

____

____

____

____

____

SIGHT WORDS

THE THE THE

NO NO NO NO

COUCH COUCH

TOUCH TOUCH

PLAY PLAY PLAY

OUT OUT OUT

GO GO GO GO

SIGHT WORDS

JUMP JUMP

HERE HERE HERE

UP UP UP

CAN CAN CAN

LOOK LOOK LOOK

SMELL SMELL

ABOUT THE AUTHOR

Selena Pyle is a born and raised Guyanese girl that has been motivated to write a book since the age of 8 . She is now a single mom at the age of 21 and chose to publish her first book in hopes of teaching young kids that it is okay for mommy to say no and to help them to understand why . Selena lived in Guyana with her mom from the ages of 6-12 and between these ages her mom told her no now she lives in Georgia and has her own baby and understands that love is easy but keeping your kids safe is hard .